Chinese Proverbs

Chinese Proverbs

TRANSLATED BY WILLIAM SCARBOROUGH

SIRIUS

SIRIUS

This edition published in 2022 by Sirius Publishing, a division of
Arcturus Publishing Limited,
26/27 Bickels Yard, 151–153 Bermondsey Street,
London SE1 3HA

ISBN: 978-1-3988-2061-6
AD010537UK

Printed in China

Contents

Introduction

(adapted from William Scarborough,
A Collection of Chinese Proverbs, 1875)

Chinese proverbs have a rich history. Idiomatic expressions in written form
have been found as far back as the Shang Dynasty (1766–1122 BCE) and
have littered the conversations of ordinary Chinese people for thousands
of generations. They take many forms – from the highly formalized four-
character *chengyu* (成语), many of which derive from ancient classical
literature such as the works of Laozi and Confucius, to the everyday wisdom
of the rural population handed down the generations, usually described as
yànyǔ (谚语).

Proverbs have been widely used in daily conversation in China, and the
conversations of ordinary Chinese people are highly seasoned with the salt
of its ancient wisdom. They add a piquancy and flavour to language, and can
convey a truth in the most terse and striking manner.

The prominence of such idioms comes especially to the fore during
Chinese Lunar New Year, when a number of admired sayings are written out
on long strips of red, orange, yellow, green or blue paper. These are affixed to
doors, to the side-posts of doors, to the pillars of houses, to the masts, stems
and sterns of ships, and indeed, to all manner of public structures. In this

way the very habitations of the Chinese become eloquent with sage maxims, felicitous sayings and well-expressed prayers.

Form

A Chinese proverb is something almost, if not utterly, indefinable. Of course it bears, in several features, a strong likeness to other branches of the proverb family in various countries; but, of 'that sententious brevity,' which is said to 'constitute the principal beauty of a proverb' – of that brevity without obscurity, which is said to be the very soul of a proverb – proverbs within other linguistic traditions can often be somewhat lacking. Other features the Chinese proverbial idiom has which are peculiarly its own, and which impart to it a terseness, beauty and symmetry.

The marvellous flexibility of the Chinese language enables it to mould itself to any whim people or custom may suggest. Its remarkable copiousness affords an almost unlimited scope in the selection of words, and its extreme conciseness fits it to express the greatest number of ideas using the fewest possible characters. Furthermore, the peculiar construction of its written characters gives it an altogether unparalleled power to play upon words.

Nothing will sooner strike one who examines a number of Chinese proverbs than the fact of their extreme diversity of form. It may seem, at first, as though there are no rules that shape them. But, just as to the eye of a skilful botanist, the promiscuous growths on the sides of a shady stream fall into ranks and classes, so to one who examines these proverbs with a little care, they will be seen to class themselves together, until, out of what seemed a perfect chaos, several orders arise.

The first and greatest law evident in the formation of Chinese proverbs is that of Parallelism. Great numbers of them take the form of couplets. This may be accounted for by the facts that couplet-making was traditionally a favourite amusement of the educated classes, and that couplets, when well-turned, were objects of intense admiration.

Of these couplet proverbs there are three kinds. The first and most important of these is the *duì zǐ* (对子) or antithetical couplet. This is formed according to strictly technical rules. A *duì zǐ* may contain any number of words, but the most frequent number is seven in each line. It must be "written [so] that the order of the tones in the first line shall be, *firstly* deflected, *secondly* even and *thirdly* deflected; in the second line, *firstly* even, *secondly* deflected and *thirdly* even; or *vice versa*. Should the first, third or fifth characters violate this rule, it is of no consequence; the second, fourth and sixth cannot be allowed to do so. It is essential also that the last character in the first line should be in a deflected tone, and the last in the second line in an even tone. The same characters may not be repeated in either line, and it is essential that there be an antithesis, as well in the sense as in the tones, of the words composing the two lines of the couplet. It is also a rule that particles must be placed in antithesis to particles; the same must be true of nouns, verbs, *etc.*, to nouns, verbs, etc.

The following example illustrates all these particulars:

天上众星皆拱牝

tiān shàng zhòng xīng jiē gǒng pìn

世间无水不朝东

shì jiān wú shuǐ bù zhāo dōng

'All the stars of heaven salute the north; all the rivers of the world flow towards the east', i.e. the Emperor is the centre of attraction.

How highly the Chinese themselves prize these *duì zǐ* may be gathered from the following story. Formerly an Imperial Examiner from Beijing, surnamed *Shé* (snake), seeing the haughty inscription over one of the entrances to the examination hall at Wuchang – 'Only the men of Huquang possess talent' – resented the statement, declaring that he would issue one line of a *duì zǐ* to which no Huquang man could write a reply. Accordingly, he issued his riddle using the following line :

七鸭浮塘数

qī yā fú táng shù

数三双一只

shù sān shuāng yī zhī

'Seven ducks floating on the pond; count as many as you can, there will only be three couples, plus one.'

On his return to Beijing, the examiner mentioned this circumstance to

Xióng Zǐgāng (熊子剛), an officer in the capital, who happened to be a Huquang man. He said, 'There are no men of talent in Huquang; I wrote a couplet line to which nobody could reply.' 'Indeed?' asked *Xióng Zǐgāng*, 'What was it you gave them?' On hearing the line given above, he guilefully replied, 'I have heard that a response has been written.' Thereupon he repeated to the astonished examiner his own impromptu line, as follows :

尺蛇出涧量

chǐ shé chū jiàn liáng

量九寸十分

liáng jiǔ cùn shí fēn

This means, 'A *snake* a foot long comes out of its hole; measure it as much as you can, it is only 11 inches and 8 eighths long.'

In this way, the Huquang man used a joke to get the better of the examiner, and at the same time vindicated his fellow provincials from the charge of stupidity.

Another category of couplet proverbs is one which the Chinese call *lián jù* (联句), or connected sentences. The proverbs in this class are exceedingly numerous; they are of various lengths, of different styles of composition, and are informal in all else but the corresponding number of words in each line. There is generally, however, a sharp antithesis between the first and second lines. One example will suffice for illustration:

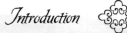

穷莫与畲长

qióng mò yǔ shē cháng;

富莫与官鬪

fù mò yǔ guān dòu

'The poor must not quarrel with the rich, nor the rich with magistrates.'

Another class of couplet proverbs focuses on rhyme — these need not be at the end of the line, but can instead be internal. Of these there are a great many which do not seem to rhyme to a foreigner; on the other hand, they may hear many rhymes where the native speaker can hear none. The explanation of this is that in order to rhyme to a native ear, the tones must correspond, while a foreigner's ear catches the ring of the rhyme. One example will suffice to show how melodiously some in this class of proverbs can chime:

好秦无好濮天下一大半

hǎo qín wú hǎo fèn tiān xià yī dà bàn

好濮无好妻　天下一夭堆

hǎo fèn wú hǎo qī tiān xià yī yāo duī

'In the great majority of cases,
Wives have fair, and husbands, ugly faces ;
But there are many, on the other side,
Where the man is bound to an ugly bride.'

We have now discussed Parallelism and its influence on the formation of proverbs and must briefly glance at those proverbs that are cast in a more irregular and prosaic mould. Among these a small number possess a kind of rhythm, which gives to the proverbs in question a very easy and flowing utterance, almost deserving for them a place along with the versified classes. An example of this is found in the following:

纽　得过人来纽　不过天

niǔ dé guò rén lái niǔ bù guò tiān

'A person can be bound, but Heaven cannot be tied down.'

The great bulk of these prose proverbs are exactly that: prosaic. Many of them consist of one plain sentence, such as 君子言前不言后 (jūn zǐ yán qián bù yán hòu) 'A leader speaks up before the event, not after it.' Many others are most irregular in shape, amply deserving the name given to them by the Chinese of 长短句 (cháng duǎn jù), or 'long and short sentences.'

Beauty of sentiment and expression are by no means rare in Chinese proverbs. Expressive of the transient character of earthly happiness, we have, 'The bright moon is not round for long; the brilliant cloud is easily scattered.' The vanity and emptiness of earthly wealth and fame could hardly be more beautifully expressed than in the following couplet:

'Wealth among men is like dew among plants:
Foam on the waves is the fame that Earth grants.'

Within this volume you will find proverbs to guide you in every aspect of life. They range from the general and metaphysical, to everyday domestic affairs and relations, to appropriate conduct in work and business. They present a unique and timeless wisdom in the vernacular Chinese that has its own charms and forms a different type of literature to that seen in the ancient classics.

A Note on the Text

Simplified characters have been used throughout this volume for ease of use, along with pinyin transliterations, as these will be most familiar to the widest number of readers. These proverbs were originally collected by William Scarborough in 1875 but have been updated and new, modern translations provided where necessary to reflect more accurately the true meanings of the proverbs for a contemporary audience.

Cause & Effect

因果关系

雷声大，雨点小

léi shēng dà, yǔ diǎn xiǎo

It thunders loudly, but rains very little

凡事必有因

fán shì bì yǒu yīn

Everything must have a cause

斩草除根，萌芽不发

zhǎn cǎo chú gēn, méng yá bù fā

Pull up the grass by the root, and it will sprout no more.

无阴

shù dǎo wú yīn

When the tree falls the shade is gone.

物各有主

wù gè yǒu zhǔ

Every thing is ruled by something.

不上高山不显平地

bù shàng gāo shān bù xiǎn píng dì

If you don't scale the mountain, you
cannot view the plain.

坐食山崩

zuò shí shān bēng

He who does nothing but sit and eat, will bring the
mountain crashing down.

从来好事必竟多磨

cóng lái hǎo shì bì jìng duō mó

A good deed always requires much work.

跟好学好

gēn hǎo xué hǎo

By following good we learn to be good.
Follow the good and learn to be so.

牵牛喝水先打湿脚

qiān niú hē shuǐ xiān dǎ shī jiǎo

He who leads an ox to drink must
first wet his own feet.

针无两头尖

zhēn wú liǎng tóu jiān

No needle has two sharp points.

一个巴掌遮不住太阳

yī gè bā zhang zhē bú zhù tài yang

One hand is not enough to block the sun.

独脚戏难唱

dú jiǎo xì nán chàng

It is difficult for one actor to perform a whole play.

万丈高楼从地起

wàn zhàng gāo lóu cóng dì qǐ

The loftiest towers rise from the ground.

慢功出细活

màn gōng chū xì huó

Slow work produces fine results.

久炼成钢

jiǔ liàn chéng gāng

Iron long fired becomes steel.

有志不在年高，

yǒu zhì bú zài nián gāo,

无志空长百岁

wú zhì kōng zhǎng bǎi suì

Resolution is independent of great age; but without
it one lives a hundred years in vain.

Home & Household

家和家庭

用尽天下只有钱好，

yòng jìn tiān xià zhī yǒu qián hǎo,

吃尽天下只有盐好

chī jìn tiān xià zhī yǒu yán hǎo

**Money and salt are the most useful
things on Earth.**

行不计路，食不计数

xíng bú jì lù, shí bú jì shù

**When travelling don't plan the route;
when eating don't count the dishes.**

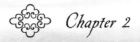

衣饭逐日生

yī fàn zhú rì shēng

Clothes and food are daily mercies.

饮食约而精,

yǐn shí yuē ér jīng,

园蔬愈珍馐

yuán shū yù zhēn xiū

Feed moderately on wholesome food;
garden herbs surpass rich viands.

桐陰秋月
清宮莞先生

野雀无粮天地宽

yě què wú liáng tiān dì kuān

When the wild bird lacks food, the whole
earth lies spread before him.

多吃少滋味，少吃多滋味

duō chī shǎo zī wèi, shǎo chī duō zī wèi

The more you eat, the less you taste
the flavour; the less you eat, the more you
savour the flavour.

人大分家，树大分桠

rén dà fēn jiā, shù dà fēn yā

Just as a grown tree spreads its branches,
so must a family divide as it grows.

要得好，老敬小

yào dé hǎo, lǎo jìng xiǎo

If you want to get along, let the old
respect the young.

一家不够，百家相凑

yī jiā bú gòu, bǎi jiā xiāng còu

Whenever one family comes to grief, a hundred
families send relief.

家丑不可外扬

jiā chǒu bù kě wài yáng

Domestic foibles must not be aired
outside the home.

国易治，家难齐

guó yì zhì, jiā nán qí

It is easier to rule a country than a family.

家和万事兴

jiā hé wàn shì xīng

In a united family happiness springs up of itself.

狗瘦主人羞

gǒu shòu zhǔ rén xiū

A lean dog brings shame on his master.

良禽择木而栖

liáng qín zé mù ér qī

A good bird selects the tree in which it nests.

远水难救近火,

yuǎn shuǐ nán jiù jìn huǒ,

远亲不如近邻

yuǎn qīn bù rú jìn lín

Distant water will not quench a nearby fire; distant relations are not so good as near neighbours.

察实莫过邻里

chá shí mò guò lín lǐ

To discover the truth about someone,
ask their neighbours.

Friends & Family

朋友和家人

若要小儿安,

ruò yào xiǎo ér ān,

三分饥与寒

sān fēn jī yǔ hán

If you want to see your children to grow up strong,
make sure they wear nor eat too much.

他养我小, 我养他老

tā yǎng wǒ xiǎo, wǒ yǎng tā lǎo

He kept my early years from care; I'll keep and
comfort his grey hair.

看儿歹好，须从幼小

kàn ér dǎi hǎo, xū cóng yòu xiǎo

One may see what a son may be from
what he is in infancy.

父不仁，子奔他乡

fù bù rén, zǐ bēn tā xiāng

When fathers are unkind, sons fly to distant shores.

养儿不知娘辛苦

yǎng ér bù zhī niáng xīn kǔ

The child knows not what trouble they
have given their mother.

龙生龙子, 凤生凤儿

lóng shēng lóng zǐ, fèng shēng fèng ér

Like father like son.
Lit: Dragons give birth to dragons,
and phoenixes hatch phoenixes.

严父出孝子

yán fù chū xiào zǐ

Strict fathers have filial sons.

父子和而家不退，

fù zǐ hé ér jiā bú tuì,

兄弟和而家不分

xiōng dì hé ér jiā bù fēn

When father and son agree, the family will not fail;
when brothers agree, the family will not fall out.

孝顺还生孝顺子,

xiào shùn huán shēng xiào shùn zǐ,

忤逆还生忤逆儿

wǔ nì huán shēng wǔ nì ér

Dutiful parents have dutiful children; undutiful parents have undutiful children.

有法治得邪，有理打得爷

yǒu fǎ zhì dé xié, yǒu lǐ dǎ dé yé

With right on his side even a son may
correct a father.

浪子回头金不换

làng zǐ huí tóu jīn bú huàn

A prodigal child's repentance is
a priceless treasure.

公不离婆，秤不离铊

gōng bù lí pó, chèng bù lí tuó

Just as a husband and wife should not be apart, so the scales should not be without their weights.

夫妻相好合，

fū qī xiāng hǎo hé,

琴瑟与笙簧

qín sè yǔ shēng huáng

Husband and wife in perfect concord are like the music of the harp and the lute.

夫妻恩厚，儿女情长

fū qī ēn hòu, ér nǚ qíng cháng

Loving husbands and wives enjoy the enduring
affection of their sons and daughters.

兄弟如手足

xiōng dì rú shǒu zú

An older brother and a young brother are like the
hands and the feet.

勿以丝毫利，

wù yǐ sī háo lì,

便伤骨肉亲

biàn shāng gǔ ròu qīn

Never allow the slightest consideration of profit to injure the affection due between those who are of the same bone and flesh.

交义不交财，

jiāo yì bù jiāo cái,

交财两不来

jiāo cái liǎng bù lái

Friendship flourishes on goodness, not on gain.

朝兄弟，暮仇敌

zhāo xiōng dì, mù chóu dí

Friends in the morning, foes at night.

人熟是宝

rén shú shì bǎo

A dear friend is a treasure.

得意忘言，无所不谈

dé yì wàng yán, wú suǒ bù tán

When friendship is real, people can
talk without reserve.

固结不可解

gù jié bù kě jiě

Those bound together cannot easily be prized apart.

相识满天下，

xiāng shí mǎn tiān xià,

知心能几人

zhī xīn néng jǐ rén

One's acquaintances must fill the world; but one's
familiar friends must be few.

乐莫乐兮新相知，

lè mò lè xī xīn xiāng zhī,

悲莫悲兮生别离

bēi mò bēi xī shēng bié lí

No joy equals that of making a new friend, no sorrow
that of being separated from friends.

对面与语，心隔千山

duì miàn yǔ yǔ, xīn gé qiān shān

Though conversing face to face, their hearts have a
thousand hills between them.

Fortune

财富

有福同享，有祸同当

yǒu fú tóng xiǎng, yǒu huò tóng dāng

Happiness we'll together share, misery we'll together bear.

医得病，医不得命

yī dé bìng, yī bù dé mìng

Disease may be cured, not fate.

心高命不高

xīn gāo mìng bù gāo

His heart is loftier than his destiny.

黄河尚有澄清日，

huáng hé shàng yǒu chéng qīng rì,

岂有人无得运时

qǐ yǒu rén wú dé yùn shí

Even the Yellow River has its clear days; how can one
be altogether without luck?

天有不测风云，

tiān yǒu bú cè fēng yún,

人有旦夕祸福

rén yǒu dàn xī huò fú

People's fortunes are as uncertain as the winds
and clouds of Heaven.

拨开浮云见青天

bō kāi fú yún jiàn qīng tiān

When the meandering clouds are dispersed
we see a clear sky.

稻草包珍珠

dào cǎo bāo zhēn zhū

A pearl wrapped up in straw.

(Note – said of able or learned persons whose ill luck
it is to live unnoticed and unknown.)

当取不取，过后莫悔

dāng qǔ bù qǔ, guò hòu mò huǐ

He who neglects a good opportunity must not
complain about it afterwards.

少壮不努力，

shào zhuàng bù nǔ lì,

大徒伤悲

lāo dà tú shāng bēi

Slackness when young leads to sorrow in old age.

借风过河

jiè fēng guò hé

Borrow the wind to cross the river.

趁热打铁

chèn rè dá tiě

Strike while the iron is hot.

Education

教育

天下之事，非教无成

tiān xià zhī shì, fēi jiào wú chéng

Nothing can be achieved without instruction.

事虽小不做不成，

shì suī xiǎo bú zuò bù chéng,

子虽贤不教不明

zǐ suī xián bú jiào bù míng

Though an affair be small, it must be attended to,
else it will never be done: though a son be talented,
without education, he will remain ignorant.

各将本事跳龙门

gè jiāng běn shì tiào lóng mén

Anyone who shows ability may leap the dragon gate,

那怕文章高天下,

nā pà wén zhāng gāo tiān xià,

试官不中也枉然

shí guān bù zhōng yě wǎng rán

**Who fears that their essay will surpass all others,
rather than the examiners will reject it?**

行患不能成，

xíng huàn bù néng chéng,

无患有司之不公

wú huàn yǒu sī zhī bù gōng

Fear the imperfection in your conduct, not the lack of honesty in your examiner.

斯文同骨肉

sī wén tóng gǔ ròu

All scholars are brethren.

诗中有画，画中有诗

shī zhōng yǒu huà, huà zhōng yǒu shī

There are paintings in poems, and poems in paintings.

一日之师，终身为父

yī rì zhī shī, zhōng shēn wéi fù

Who teaches me for a day is a father for life.

自古书有味，

zì gǔ shū yǒu wèi,

砚田无恶岁

yàn tián wú è suì

Books provide succour; the printed page
knows no famine.

黄金有价书无价

huáng jīn yǒu jià shū wú jià

Learning is far more precious than gold.

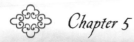

千般易学，一窍难通

qiān bān yì xué, yī qiào nán tōng

Most things are easy to learn but hard to master.

开卷有益

kāi juàn yǒu yì

You cannot open a book without learning something.

读书如流水

dú shū rú liú shuǐ

Your study goes on like a flowing stream.

读书须用意，

dú shū xū yòng yì,

一字值千金

yī zì zhí qiān jīn

Be diligent in study, for every word is worth a thousand gold coins.

学然后知不足

xué rán hòu zhī bù zú

Studying breeds a thirst for more.

三日不读书，

sān rì bù dú shū,

便觉语言无味

biàn jué yǔ yán wú wèi

Three days without study leaves one's conversation flavourless.

书乃随身之宝

shū nǎi suí shēn zhī bǎo

Learning is a treasure which follows its owner everywhere.

最乐莫如读书为善

zuì lè mò rú dòu shū wéi shàn

No pleasure equals the pleasure of study.

Joy & Sorrow

喜悦与悲伤

一人有福，托带满屋

yī rén yǒu fú, tuō dài mǎn wū

One man in a house, of joy possessed, passes it on to all the rest.

人寿年丰节气和

rén shòu nián fēng jié qì hé

May you live long, your years be plenteous and your seasons felicitous!

乐极生悲

lè jí shēng bēi

Bliss gives birth to sorrow.

明月不常圆，

míng yuè bù cháng yuán,

彩云容易散

cǎi yún róng yì sàn

Happiness is transient.
Lit.: The bright moon is not round for long;
brilliant clouds are easily scattered.

前人栽树，后人乘凉

qián rén zāi shù, hòu rén chéng liáng

One generation plants the trees under whose cool
shade another generation rests.

但能守本分，

Dàn néng shǒu běn fèn,

终身无烦恼

zhōng shēn wú fán nǎo

Those who take their share of responsibility shall lead trouble-free lives.

黄金未为贵，

huáng jīn wèi wéi guì,

安乐值钱多

ān lè zhí qián duō

Peace and joy are more precious than gold.

福至心灵

fú zhì xīn líng

Happiness makes the mind nimbler.

知足者贫贱亦乐，

zhī zú zhě pín jiàn yì lè,

不知足者贵富亦忧

bù zhī zú zhě fù guì yì yōu

To the contented even poverty and obscurity bring happiness; to the discontented even riches and honours bring misery.

生离死别，悲哀最切

shēng lí sǐ bié, bēi āi zuì qiè

Apart living and parted dying, no grief on earth can be so trying.

人欺天勿欺，

rén qī tiān wù qī,

吃亏就是便宜

chī kuī jiù shì pián yi

People may despise me, but if Heaven does not, suffering is an agreeable lot.

所乐者浅，所患者深

suǒ lè zhě qiǎn, suǒ huàn zhě shēn

Our pleasures are shallow, our troubles deep.

才离狼窝，又入虎口

cái lí láng wō, yòu rù hǔ kǒu

Out of the wolf's den, into the tiger's mouth.

惹祸招灾，问罪应该

rě huò zhāo zāi, wèn zuì yīng gāi

Whoever provokes misfortune and distress deserves
to suffer for their foolishness.

害人终害己

hài rén zhōng hài jǐ

When you harm others, you harm yourself.

一龙阻住千江水

yì lóng zǔ zhù qiān jiāng shuǐ

One person may obstruct many.
Lit.: One dragon may block a thousand rivers.

人生在世如春梦，

rén shēng zài shì rú chūn mèng,

灵魂一走万事休

líng hún yì zǒu wàn shì xiū

Our life on Earth is like a dream in Spring; once the
soul has fled, all things take their rest.

Manners

礼仪

不知好歹，岂识高低

bù zhī hǎo dǎi, qǐ shí gāo dī

Those who have no morals know no manners.

长幼内外，宜法肃辞严

cháng yòu nèi wài, yí fǎ sù cí yán

Old or young, male or female, all should speak and
behave with respect.

人恶礼不恶

rén è lǐ bú è

A wicked person may have good manners.

以情还情

yǐ qíng huán qíng

Return gift for gift.

宁可慢客，不可饿客

nìng kě màn kè, bù kě è kè

Better slight a guest than starve them.

客来主不顾，

kè lái zhǔ bú gù,

应恐是痴人

yīng kǒng shì chī rén

The person who does not warmly welcome
guests is a fool.

宴客切勿留连

yàn kè qiè wù liú lián

One should entertain guests but not insist they stay.

Business

经商

二人同一心,

èr rén tóng yì xīn,

黄土变成金

huáng tǔ biàn chéng jīn

When two partners are of one mind, clay
is into gold refined.

利大害大

lì dà hài dà

Great profits bring great risks.

漫天要价, 就地还钱

mán tiān yào jià, jiù dì huán qián

When the price one asks for costs the stars, the
money one receives comes down to earth.

价高招远客

jià gāo zhāo yuǎn kè

High prices attract sellers from afar.

小生意赚大钱

xiǎo shēng yi zhuàn dà qián

Small businesses make great profit.

忍嘴不欠债

rěn zuǐ bú qiàn zhài

He who controls his appetite avoids debt.

跑得了和尚跑不了庙

páo dé liǎo hé shàng páo bù liǎo miào

The priest may run away, but the temple cannot.

百艺无如一艺精

bǎi yì wú rú yí yì jīng

It is better to be a master of one skill than a Jack-of-all-trades.

隔行如隔山

gé háng rú gé shān

Every man to his calling.
Lit.: Separate trades are like separate hills.

同道者相爱,

tóng dào zhě xiāng ài,

同艺者相嫉

tóng yì zhě xiāng jí

Philosophers share a mutual love, artists share a mutual jealousy.

管山的烧柴,

guǎn shān de shāo chái,

管河的吃水

guǎn hé de chī shuǐ

Who keeps the hills, burns the wood; who keeps the stream, drinks the water.

Morality

道德

岂能尽如人意，

qǐ néng jìn rú rén yì,

但求无愧我心

dàn qiú wú kuì wǒ xīn

Since we can never fully please others, let us seek merely to satisfy our own conscience.

欺心折尽平生福，

qī xīn zhé jìn píng shēng fú,

行短天教一世贫

xíng duǎn tiān jiào yí shì pín

Cheat your conscience and a whole life's happiness is destroyed; let your conduct be faulty and Heaven will teach you a lifelong lesson in poverty.

为善则流芳百世

wéi shàn zé liú fāng bǎi shì

The fragrance of virtuous conduct will last for a hundred generations.

但行好事，莫问前程

dàn xíng hǎo shì, mò wèn qián chéng

Do good regardless of the consequences.

勿以恶小而为之，

wù yǐ è xiǎo ér wéi zhī,

勿以善小而不为

wù yǐ shàn xiǎo ér bù wéi

Do not practice vice, however trivial; do not abandon virtue, however small.

修道虽无人见，

xiū dào suī wú rén jiàn,

存心自有天知

cún xīn zì yǒu tiān zhī

Although the right path may be invisible to others, a
true heart will be recognized in Heaven.

说好不为好，

shuō hǎo bù wéi hǎo,

做好方为好

zuò hǎo fāng wéi hǎo

To say you have done good is not goodness;
but to do good is.

无事不可对人言

wú shì bù kě duì rén yán

There is nothing one can do that others cannot be told about.

下坡容易上坡难

xià pō róng yi shàng pō nán

It is easier to run down a hill than up one.

人不劝不善，

rén bú quàn bú shàn,

钟不打不鸣

zhōng bù dǎ bù míng

One will not be virtuous without exhortation, just
like a bell will not sound if it is not struck.

见死不救，一行大罪

jiàn sǐ bù jiù, yī xíng dà zuì

To refuse to save a life is one of the greatest crimes.

135

要得好，问三老

yào dé hǎo, wèn sān lǎo

If to be right is your desire, then of three old men
you should enquire.

贤不责愚

xián bù zé yú

A wise man will not reprove a fool.

君有臣谏，父有子谏

jūn yǒu chén jiàn, fù yǒu zǐ jiàn

Princes have censors — fathers, sons that
reprove them.

甘言疾也，苦言药也

gān yán jí yě, kǔ yán yào yě

Flattery is a sickness; reproof is a medicine.

责人之心责己，

zé rén zhī xīn zé jǐ,

恕己之心恕人

shù jǐ zhī xīn shù rén

Blame yourself as you would blame others; excuse others as you would yourself.

先正自己，后正他人

xiān zhèng zì jǐ, hòu zhèng tā rén

First put yourself right, then others.

道吾好者是吾贼，

dào wú hǎo zhě shì wú zéi,

道吾恶者是吾师

dào wú è zhě shì wú shī

The one who flatters me is my enemy – the one who reproves me is my teacher.

色不迷人人自迷

sè bù mí rén rén zì mí

It is not beauty that beguiles people; people
beguile themselves.

说大话用小钱

shuō dà huà yòng xiǎo qián

To promise much and give little.

鹬蚌相持，渔人得利

yù bàng xiāng chí, yú rén dé lì

When the heron and oyster quarrelled, it was the
fisherman who benefitted.

大事化小，小事化无

dà shì huà xiǎo, xiǎo shì huà wú

Convert great quarrels into small ones, and small
ones into nothing.

事怕当面

shì pà dāng miàn

When men come face to face, their
differences vanish.

贪图小利，难成大事

tān tú xiǎo lì, nán chéng dà shì

He who covets small profits will struggle to make
great transactions.

莫道君行早,

mò dào jūn xíng zǎo,

有早行人

gēng yǒu zǎo xíng rén

Don't boast of being first, for there will be many others in front of you.

耳不听, 心不烦

ěr bù tīng, xīn bù fán

When the ear does not hear, the heart does not grieve.

自己有错, 休怪别人

zì jǐ yǒu cuò, xiū guài bié ren

Don't blame others for your own faults.

偷得利而后有害

tōu dé lì ér hòu yǒu hài

Nothing in the end is gained by stealing.

停手就停口

tíng shǒu jiù tíng kǒu

He who will not work shall not eat.

慈悲为本，方便为门

cí bēi wéi běn, fāng biàn wéi mén

Mercy is the root and core; opportunity the door.

从善如登，从恶如崩

cóng shàn rú dēng, cóng è rú bēng

Following virtue is an ascent steep; following vice a precipitous leap.

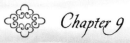

重仁义轻死亡

zhòng rén yì qīng sǐ wáng

Kindness and duty should be important; death should be inconsequential.

善乃福之基,

shàn nǎi fú zhī jī,

恶乃祸之兆

è nǎi huò zhī zhào

Virtue is the foundation of happiness, vice the harbinger of misery.

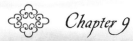

能忍一时之气，

néng rěn yì shí zhī qì,

免得百日之忧

miǎn dé bǎi rì zhī yōu

Forbearance of a slight provocation may save one a hundred days' trouble.

孝心感动天和地

xiào xīn gǎn dòng tiān hé dì

Filial piety moves Heaven and Earth.

常舍常有，富贵长久

cháng shě cháng yǒu, fù guì cháng jiǔ

Those who give always receive; their riches and honours last forever.

人情大过王法

rén qíng dà guò wáng fǎ

Human kindness exceeds royal prerogative.

施惠勿念，受恩莫忘

shī huì wù niàn, shòu ēn mò wàng

Be forgetful of favours given; be mindful of blessings received.

饮水思源

yǐn shuǐ sī yuán

When you drink from the stream,
remember the spring.

Prudence

谨慎

日防风浪之险,

rì fáng fēng làng zhī xiǎn,

夜防盗贼之忧

yè fáng dào zéi zhī yōu

Beware of winds and waves by day, of
thieves by night.

差之毫厘, 失之千里

chā zhī háo lí, shī zhī qiān lǐ

Deviate an inch and you lose a thousand miles.

风平浪未静

fēng píng làng wèi jìng

Though the wind has fallen the waves have not yet settled.

人狼不逢，酒狠不喝

rén hěn bù féng, jiū hěn bù hē

Avoid fierce men and strong wine.

到哪里说哪里话

dào nǎ lǐ shuō nǎ lǐ huà

Wherever you go, talk as the people of that place talk.

钱不错用，工无枉使

qián bú cuò yòng, gōng wú wǎng shǐ

Neither spend foolishly, nor work fruitlessly.

输赢无悔

shū yíng wú huǐ

Neither victory nor loss should cause regret.

量体裁衣

liáng tǐ cái yī

Cut your cloth according to your measure.

饮水知源

yǐn shuǐ zhī yuán

If you drink the water you'll know the spring.

口说不如身逢

kǒu shuō bù rú shēn féng

There are no words that can match individual
experience.

眼瞎路熟

yǎn xiā lù shú

Though the traveller may be blind,

they know the road.

草不除根，终当复生

cǎo bù chú gēn, zhōng dāng fù shēng

Grass not dug up by the roots will again send forth its shoots.